D1548631

Euclid Public Library
631 E. 222nd Street
Euclid, Ohio 44123
216-261-5300

from CLASSIC *to* CONTEMPORARY

from CLASSIC to CONTEMPORARY

DECORATING WITH CULLMAN & KRAVIS

ELISSA CULLMAN AND TRACEY PRUZAN

THE MONACELLI PRESS

CONTENTS

INTRODUCTION

I grew up in a modest home in Brooklyn long before it was the epicenter of cool. My mother was a business-woman who had no interest in interior design, but she always kept our house in immaculate order, well maintained, and up-to-date. As for antiques, she thought they were most definitely for people who could not afford new furniture. In comparison, I was always drawn to the field of interior design, and I was especially fascinated by antique furniture and objects, although I'm not really sure why.

I was not lucky enough to have formal training as a designer of any kind, but by the time I was thirty, my passionate interest in history, the two years I spent in Japan when I was first married, and the very practical necessity of decorating our first home undeniably led me toward a career as a decorator. When my best friend, Hedi Kravis, and I started our firm in 1984, we felt confident that we understood both the aesthetic and practical applications of our newfound careers. Armed with John Cornforth's seminal book, *The Inspiration of the Past*, and inspired by the ongoing business success of the iconic firm of Colefax and Fowler, we set forth to conquer the field, proclaiming proudly that form and function were the twin pillars of interior design.

Over the past thirty plus years, Cullman & Kravis has grown to a staff of eighteen, with projects ranging from New York City to Houston, from the Hamptons to Miami, from Nantucket to Maui. We have been so lucky to be recognized within our industry, with projects published by *Architectural Digest, Elle Decor, Veranda, House Beautiful, Luxe, Cottages & Gardens,* and more. I couldn't be happier about the firm's accomplishments and want to thank my brilliantly talented staff, past and present, and especially my four partners—Lee Cavanaugh, Sarah Ramsey, Claire Ratliff, and Alyssa Urban—for their enormous contribution to the success of our business. I couldn't be prouder, but at the same time I am humbled and inspired.

At the end of the day, what has made interior design so fascinating for me is that it has been a perpetual learning experience. Almost ten years ago, Tracey Pruzan and I wrote *Decorating Master Class* to provide a comprehensive look at the "big picture" by exploring all the rules and basics of design. More recently, we wrote *The Detailed Interior* to look at the small things, to see what makes our work look so complete, layered and most distinctive. The question now is, why another book? And why now?

Today we live in a world of websites, shelter magazines, and how-to books. We're bombarded with one-line style tips for do-it-your-selfers on the one hand and, on the other, we're teased with unattainable glossy photographs of the interiors of the rich and famous. How can someone make sense of all the options? In this book, we want to show you that the best approach is to return to those foundations of design that we explored in *Decorating Master Class*, except that now our goal is to redefine traditional interiors with a modern perspective, while in our more contemporary projects, the classic principles of design guide our process.

There is an evolution happening in design, and our expectations and demands are changing at an incredible speed. The push for all things modern is streamlining the way people live, work, and play. Our whole world is moving toward the aesthetic of clean lines, and you can see it in our super-thin TV screens and the personal computers on our wrists. Interiors have to follow suit, shedding some layers, becoming leaner and more contemporary as conditions demand. We want curtains without heavy valances and swags, furniture without skirts and fringe, art displayed without heavy frames. The de-cluttered lines of our up-to-the-minute lives have actually changed the way we live and affected our expectations about interior design.

But when we embrace a more up-to-date look, we don't have to suddenly design with minimal black leather and chrome. Good design is still about proportion, composition, and a balanced range of colors, materials, and textures that you respond to, no matter your age or personal style. To design interiors that feel relevant today, we stand by our commitments to the foundations of design.

In the pages that follow, you'll see modest revisions, complete renovations, and ground-up projects. We will share an up-close and personal account of what we've done in each of the interiors to make them more contemporary. In all, we hope you'll see how we embrace a suave historicism with exciting new takes on tradition, referencing a wide range of cultures and contemporary design motifs. And, most importantly, we hope you will be able to approach your own decorating projects with a newly educated appreciation and understanding for all of these topics. It's a lot to learn, a lot to think about, and a lot to do. So let's get started!

AT HOME

There's something I love about experimenting at home. When you spend your life designing for others, your home becomes a laboratory, a place to take risks that you might not with a client's home.

This apartment has been my home for thirty years. I raised my children here, and now they visit with my grandchildren. The apartment has been published before in magazines and also in our first book, *Decorating Master Class*, but now it's been redone, and, as I like to say, "It's your mother in a new dress."

While I have redecorated more than once (an understatement for anyone who has followed my career!), this incarnation is without doubt one of the most interesting iterations of the Cullman & Kravis approach. I want to start with it as a case study as it embodies some exciting lessons and numerous examples of the wide variety of ways you can renew, modernize, and re-invigorate. The bones are the same, but it's fresh and up-to-date, and it clearly represents the journey of my personal decorating style.

Although a full gut renovation was done ten years ago, I recently felt the rooms looked dated and a little too dark and serious. Light spaces and clean lines feel right for today. When you redecorate any room, there is always going to be a chain reaction. When you change one thing, what happens to the rest? Where do you stop and when do you keep going? There aren't any hard and fast rules, but I certainly have used this apartment to explore the answers.

A rug is the one piece in any home, in any room, about which all other decisions orbit. Its style, pattern, content, and colors set the stage, especially the living room rug, which is really the linchpin for the whole process. While searching for a new rug, I came across a gorgeous Keshan with a red ground and a sky-blue and beige motif. I knew immediately that this calmer, lighter rug would be a perfect replacement for my Bijar, which was more heavily patterned and richly saturated with a traditional palette.

If you change the rug, you need to be prepared to make other, possibly major, changes, and I was excited to see what would happen here.

OPPOSITE AND OVERLEAF: In the living room today, the cream-colored fabric on the sofas is a nubby tweed with metallic thread that reminds me of a classic Chanel suit fabric. With narrow arms and without bullion trim, the sofas look stylish and new. Instead of tassel fringes, which can feel too traditional now, we used simple cords and contrast welts on almost all the pillows and upholstery.

LEFT AND OPPOSITE: My living room in its first incarnation before the red walls, with swags and jabots at the windows, bullion fringe on the sofa, and a George III camelback settee. Nineteenth- and early twentieth-century paintings hang in the traditional envelope. OVERLEAF: We had to find two paintings that could hang side by side and thought that these works by Helen Frankenthaler and Pat Steir made an excellent pair. It's tremendously important when you're decorating to be able to envision how things might live alongside each other.

The first thing that my colleagues and I realized was that this rug would allow me to keep the wall color. That was a huge relief as the walls are a custom painted-stucco finish in my favorite shade of red. But the curtains, which in palette and style are always closely related to the rug, would definitely have to be changed, as would a few key pieces of upholstery.

The new ivory-silk curtain panels feel cooler and less fussy than the swags and jabots from before, and the pale color contrasts well with the walls. The sleek metal hardware is more modern than the original gilded wooden poles. For the upholstery, my colleagues found new fabrics glimmering with metallic threads, a welcome change from the existing velvets and silk damasks. One suggested that we thin out sofa arms and exchange curved legs for straight. Her suggestions were spot-on because with more neutral fabrics, lively colors like the red walls feel renewed and more impactful now.

Instead of buying new decorative objects and accessories, I culled the existing collections, much to the delight of my children who worry that their own kids will knock something over. With fewer objects, each feels more sculptural, and the old-school sensory overload gives way to the beauty of every piece.

There is something about emphasizing a single example—a lamp, a vase, a sculpture—that feels like a new way of seeing because you slow down and focus on the quality of the object. With fewer antique decorative objects in the rooms, the lamps and mirrors that I did purchase to replace the very traditional forms pop a feeling of modernity into the landscape. For example, if I had allowed the massing of collections to remain on the side tables, the new twentieth-century bronze-and-glass lamps from Willy Rizzo would look out of place. Conversely, if I hadn't changed the lamps, the new tailored curtains we designed would look as if they had come from another universe.

The apartment now feels refreshed, but it still feels like me. No matter what we talked about and tried out from room to room over the process, the three "sacred cows" that I never touched were the wallpaper in the dining room, the screen in the living room, and my beloved art collection. These are the things that tell the most about my family and who we are, where we've been, what we love. Whether you are redecorating or starting from scratch, don't discard the pieces you love the most. If you like something, there must be some connection that you might not be able to express, but somehow it just works. In the end, I kept more than I changed, but it still feels new, and it feels right for me—and right for today.

ABOVE AND RIGHT: The older version of my dining room seems dark and enclosed, in comparison to the new design. Now, the room is all about capturing light. The ceiling is glazed in a high-gloss varnish, and the chandelier is filled with crystals. The large nineteenth-century mirror over the sideboard, designed in the manner of William Kent, adds more light than the eighteenth-century convex mirror we hung earlier.

Two views of the library, as it used to look (left) and newly redone. It's easy to see that even in a fairly traditional room like this one, we are big believers in the wonder of white. In most rooms, we specify the wood moldings, or the ceiling, or the curtains, or pillows to be white. It's like taking a breath when you look around the room. The walls are triple-glazed in blue with an over glaze of gold to be luminous and lively.

Moving away from all the wood in the older version of the room, the new coffee table has a custom metal base and a top made of woven strips of white metal under glass. At the window, the pair of desk chairs adds eight legs into the room, so it was important that the desk have a pedestal or a column base like this one instead of four more legs. I also love the dialogue between the American trompe l'oeil painting above the desk and the Kenneth Noland target painting over the sofa.

22

DOWNTOWN ECLECTIC

After thirty years in suburbia, our clients were more than ready to return to New York City, and to somewhere downtown, where they first met and married. With a desire to move away from the traditional style of their Connecticut home, they looked in new buildings with sleek interiors. Determined to push their comfort zone, they hoped to apply a bold palette and to adopt an energetic mix of furniture and objects from vintage finds to contemporary custom pieces.

They were thrilled to discover this penthouse in a recently completed luxury complex in Greenwich Village. The apartment has the ideal combination of airy loft-style living and modern luxuries. Bronze window walls with floor-to-ceiling exposures capture the downtown edge while the rooms maintain an uptown architectural structure. Bedrooms are well-proportioned rectangles with windows and good exposures. The living room and dining area has an open floor plan, but there is also a traditional entrance hall with a powder room, and there are no exposed columns to contend with. The penthouse has the added attraction of sweeping views to the north, west, and south from the deeply set-back terraces.

Architect Oscar Shamamian was brought in to personalize the space. Within the beautifully designed interiors, our clients wanted to customize the master bedroom, the closets, and the cabinetry in the living room, adding a layer of detail and a finishing touch to the interior. They also asked for a built-in wall of refrigeration in the kitchen to accommodate their wine collection. In a sense, Shamamian was adding jewelry to an already great ensemble.

The rooms are filled with an unconventional range of furniture styles that creates a harmonious blend. Custom pieces, such as the metal-edged mahogany dining room table, which was handmade in Brooklyn, and the living room coffee table with its gleaming metal base, feel very current and chic. Purchased at the Paris flea market, the Anglo-Indian Calamander wood campaign chest from 1837 hints at travel and distant worlds.

OPPOSITE: The high-gloss paint on the entry ceiling emphasizes the ten-foot ceiling height in this industrial-style building from the 1920s. Benches covered in blue pony skin add not just a shot of color, but also a change in texture from the glowing metals, the glass table, and the reflective ceiling.
OVERLEAF: The living room is a loft-like space with an office area, a game table, and a large dining area.

One of the most fulfilling aspects of designing a room is the process in which we evaluate the scale and composition of furniture and objects to create a cohesive and beautiful environment. This can be a challenge when shopping the Marché aux Puces in Paris or at any market or antique dealer for that matter, especially if the furniture is piled high in a cluttered space. Do not hesitate to ask a dealer to move the piece you're considering away from where it's sitting. Seeing it against a plain wall or out in the open or even adjacent to a piece similar to one you already own is invaluable.

Instead of starting with the rugs as we often do, in this case we looked first to the owners' collection of photography and contemporary art, which was acquired specifically for the space. It was a collaborative process for the owners, who agreed that they both must love every purchase. Major works include paintings by Alex Katz and David Salle and photographs by Thomas Struth and Andreas Gursky.

The powerful collection inspired us to use strong colors, textures, and streamlined profiles on the furniture and the curtains, but not on the walls or the rugs. New, subtly patterned area rugs and plain painted, not patterned or glazed, walls in almost every room help ward off visual cacophony and create an uncluttered backdrop for the furniture and the art. New rugs and plain paint are also ideal for achieving instant gratification (and for moving up your installation date!) For accents, we sourced fabrics with refined ethnic designs like the vintage Suzani throw or the woven ikat print that mingle comfortably with mohair, linen, and silk upholstery.

Altogether it's an elegant combination of refinement, downtown chic, and a lot of soul in this new abode.

In the corner of the living room is one of the banes of traditional decorating: the corner glass window, so beloved in modern architecture. Instead of a vivid wall color, we stacked these forest-green wool curtains asymmetrically to maximize the city view.

LEFT: A Robert Longo digital pigment print hangs over a Calamander wood campaign chest with unusual silver mounts. RIGHT: In the dining area, the asymmetrical arrangement of the lights on pulleys references the industrialist vibe of the apartment, and they subtly separate the dining area from the connecting living room. The unexpected reflection on the table of the art glass on the sideboard changes with the light, making its own abstract image.

OPPOSITE: We lacquered the office nook bookcases in steel gray and applied glass to the backs of the shelves. The gauffrage chair fabric has a striped geometric design.
RIGHT: The powder room walls are venetian stucco painted in aubergine. The white chalk letters look abstract, but they are actually a list of all the places the owners have lived since they met.

33

One of the important design messages in the apartment was mixing wood, painted finishes, and vibrant color, all of which come together in the kitchen. Part of the kitchen, the family room is large and welcoming with an L-shaped sofa upholstered in a very durable wine-colored mohair. To the right of the sofa is a wooden breakfast table and peacock-blue lacquer chairs.

The kitchen opens to the terrace with wide glass-paned doors. We customized the white cabinetry with a painted-glass backsplash and Italian blown-glass light fixtures over the island. The forty-foot-long terrace is open to the north and west with cinematic city views.

ABOVE: The small foyer needed a transparent "hello" piece, like this table, which is also a sculptural homage to Giacometti. The mirror reflects natural light from the kitchen, opening up the narrow space. RIGHT: We fell in love with this writing table after seeing it in a photograph. The geodesic orbs and the kidney shape proved to be the missing piece of sculpture for this corner of the master bedroom. The turquoise chaise is upholstered in a custom gauffrage velvet.

In the master bedroom, the wood-framed platform bed is stylistically sympathetic to the loft-like space. The thread colors and motifs in the sheeting we design are always integral to our schemes, adding to the layering of imagery and palette in the bedrooms.

OPPOSITE: We brought the sea of stone and cabinetry in the large bathroom to life with decorative pieces like the Italian chandelier, the vintage Fornasetti chair, and the large photograph of a watery landscape. RIGHT: Her custom closet is painted all one color: a glossy Hermes shade of orange. A chinoiserie style vintage La Barge eglomisé mirror frame, a Fontana d 'Arte light fixture, and Italian sconces from the 1960s add the finishing touches. OVERLEAF: The boys' rooms are sumptuously furnished with flea market finds, including vintage leather chairs, a pair of chests with colored glass fronts, and both pairs of bedside lamps.

43

TRADITIONAL CHIC

There are some people who absolutely love traditional furnishings to the exclusion of everything else. The beauty of antique rugs, furniture, and densely patterned fabrics appeals to many of our clients, but what to do when they also love and want to live with modern art? It's a question and challenge for us to be sure, but I believe we have found the sweet spot in this Manhattan apartment where we have succeeded in integrating prewar architecture with a dynamic interior to create an environment that is sympathetic to the contemporary art.

This duplex apartment had remarkable bones including 10-foot ceilings and a generous 5,500 square feet of living space. Most unique for the city, the entrance spills into an enormous stair hall with its own skylight, almost equal in size to the footprint of the foyer, to flood the vaulted space with light. All of the rooms are substantial in size, especially the living room, which has a working fireplace and two seating areas, and the dining room, which seats twenty comfortably.

For every classic gesture, there is a more contemporary response. While we chose multicolored antique rugs for the living and dining rooms, we turned away from the multicolored patterned fabrics like chintz that we would have selected years ago. Instead, we limited the palette of the silks, velvets, and taffetas to shades of red and gold to suggest a more up-to-date vibe.

One of the most interesting aspects of planning this apartment was the scale of the art. In a more traditional space, we would have hung smaller scale or easel-size art above the chair rails and wainscoting. Those elements in turn would suggest different wall finishes above and below ranging from wood to wallpaper, all of which would be appropriate and expected in this kind of prewar architecture. But knowing that the art collection would be over-scaled gave us the opportunity to keep the walls unobstructed by moldings and painted rather than paneled wherever possible.

OPPOSITE: In this architecturally grand entrance hall, the interior design is all about bold strokes. The broad curve of the stair and the two-by-two-foot grid of the marble floor called for a dramatic grouping of masterworks like these paintings by Sean Scully, Adolph Gottlieb, and Giorgio Cavallon. OVERLEAF: A jewel-toned Sultanabad carpet sets up a classic red-and-yellow palette in the living room. A Franz Kline painting hangs over the Regency-inspired mantel.

We used an unobtrusive, cream-colored venetian stucco in the entrance hall as it would be discreet and welcoming to a collection of modern art like this one, yet more domestic and less gallery-like than pure white. Moving from room to room, we glazed the walls in the client's favorite colors—shades of red and gold—and adjusted the recipe for each in adjacent spaces to avoid repetition.

In the entry gallery, large-scale paintings seem to float up the reflective staircase walls, illuminated by the enormous skylight. Rather than the typical stair runner on dark floors, which would have absorbed light, lightly stained oak stair risers are inset with a faux bronze painted, neoclassically inspired motif. Although the idea for this luxe detail came from a historic home featured on "Downton Abbey," here it feels cool and new. Taking something rooted in history out of its original context lets you see it with a new perspective, and including it here adds to the deliberate balance of past and present.

Removing the anticipated details like ornate moldings and wall paneling from this majestic prewar apartment gave us the ideal canvas for showcasing the collection of abstract modern paintings, which now co-exists in an unexpectedly natural and harmonious way with the more traditional furnishings and antiques.

RIGHT: In the family sitting room, we selected classic red lacquered walls and a textured area rug. Printed paisley fabric on the sofa is very forgiving and will stand up to use in an informal family space. Murano glass lamps, with no metal or wood trim, add a clean look. Two-tiered coffee tables are a C&K favorite for display of books and family albums.

PRECEDING PAGES: We often use period sets of chairs and period chandeliers in dining rooms because they are hard to replicate. These chairs are English Regency and the crystal chandelier is English, c. 1870. Conversely, the cabinets flanking the fireplace and the three-pedestal table were custom designed. Red-glazed walls like these are warmly inviting all day and especially dramatic at night, and the rich color complements paintings by Robert Motherwell, over the mantel, and by Lee Krasner.

RIGHT: Less desnsely patterned than other rugs, the white-ground Tabriz provides relief from the rich Anigre wood paneling in the library.

In the master bedroom, a luscious and creamy palette prevails. At the 12-foot long window, simple curtain panels keep the view open, while the sculpture by Manierre Dawson animates the center.

OPPOSITE: To meet a hectic family and entertaining schedule, the kitchen incorporates the most durable materials we could provide. Granite, used for these countertops, is the only material guaranteed against lemon, wine, and other stains. RIGHT AND OVERLEAF: The wrap-around terrace has a full outdoor kitchen and a dining table that seats fourteen people comfortably. Designed by Hollander Design Landscape Architects, the space can hold more than one hundred people for outdoor parties.

LIVING IN COLOR

Designing for a young couple in Miami was an exciting and inspiring opportunity, especially since the family wanted to fill the space with vivid colors and bold prints that would reference the location but not feel too typically Miami.

The five-bedroom villa is distinguished by floor-to-ceiling sliding glass windows throughout. Our charge was to create glamorous entertaining spaces that would also be very functional, with ample seating and storage. Bedrooms for the kids, a playroom, and a library were all part of the program.

Before we could decorate, there was work to do. Who has bought a house that doesn't need some tweaking? Often clients want to add eye-catching details and custom amenities to make a new home feel unique. We invited our frequent collaborator Tom Kligerman to add distinctive cabinetry that would elevate and personalize the spaces. In the library, for example, he designed a luminous wall of cabinetry in polished bronze with glass shelves and drawer interiors lacquered in bright orange.

To achieve the bright and vivid feeling the clients requested, we minimized stained-wood finishes throughout. The floors are patinated a grayish-driftwood color, and the boarded ceilings are similarly toned. Most of the furniture is lacquered, bleached, or wrapped in fabric. But how to introduce color? As there were no traditional crown moldings, baseboards, and door surrounds, the usual stopping and starting points for wallpaper and paint were not present. This gave us a unique opportunity to try something new.

Instead of painting an entire room in one color as we usually do, we blocked it out within the rooms, sometimes on just one wall, sometimes all over. This animated the decorating in a very energetic way that satisfied the client's goals. In the entry, a single bold lemon-yellow wall is like a vertical welcome mat. In the living room, a lacquered band of orange paint wraps around the white walls just above and below eye level to frame the views and the art. In the master bathroom, the ceiling glows turquoise, and in a little girl's bedroom, translucent squares of sherbet-toned paint overlap and change.

This modern Miami villa is all about moments of color. In the entry, we broke with traditional C&K hallmarks by painting one wall white and the other yellow, as reflected in the mirror. A pair of Billy Haines chairs is upholstered in silver leather in homage to the owner's grandmother, the fashion icon Betsy Bloomingdale, an LA style setter whose homes were decorated by Haines in the 1950s.

The living room is dominated by the five-foot round mirror-finish sculpture, which serves as a foil to the strong rectilinear architecture. We continued to play on the idea of curves with the carpet design, the sofa, and the chaise.

64

We carried the idea of bold planes of color into the fabrics and other furnishings as well. A pair of yellow-lacquer toy-cabinet end tables punctuates the peacock-blue sofa and rug in the kitchen sitting area. The playroom wall features a rainbow of colored shelves and storage niches. The black-lacquer dining room chairs are upholstered in gray flannel on the fronts and bright yellow cashmere on the backs, just for punctuation. The large dining table top was custom designed with inlaid bands of bronze to visually break up the wooden surface.

The glass window walls were also a great inspiration, especially for the lighting, art, and accessories, where translucence and glass are recurring themes. An art-glass piece by Vetro Vero sits on the entry table, and glass bowls by Nouvel studio enhance the dining room table. Celestial glass discs by Abby Modell hang over the master bed.

For those of us living with harsh winters, there is always the fantasy of moving into a brand-new home in a warm climate with glass walls and abundant natural light. In the dead of winter, the idea of a home in the South gleaming with color and reflective surfaces sounds like heaven. And in the summer, the bright surfaces are just as refreshing, especially when you have great outdoor spaces to enjoy as well. Inside and out, this home is one to enjoy in every season.

RIGHT: In every project, the mix of upholstery styles is a critical matter. The range of shapes, materials, and edging designs as well as the shape and finish of the legs or skirt details set the mood. In this living room, the sculptural furniture forms and the horizontal channel stitching on the chaise were all carefully orchestrated to feel very contemporary. OVERLEAF: The table is the only solid wood piece in the room and we embellished it with an abstraction of inlaid brass strips. The fractured lines of the sideboard echo the linear design of the table and of the bronze chandelier. The carpet is hand tufted wool and silk in shades of yellow, gray, and cream.

ABOVE: In this Florida interpretation of a man cave, understated, cozy materials contrast with metallic and hard-edged surfaces. OPPOSITE: The lightly patterned rug is silk and wool, and the sofa fabric is an informal orange and gray woven chenille. The custom side tables are finished in a chromelike iridescent paint, and the rivets on the side chairs evoke machinery and cars. Transparent curtain panels soften the strong lines of the windows.

ABOVE: The combined family room and kitchen has a custom installation of jacks from Kaiser Sudan of Next Step Studio on the wall. The toy-storage cabinets are yellow lacquer with metal fronts. The chairs are upholstered in wipe-able faux shagreen vinyl. OPPOSITE: Kitchens with high ceilings present an opportunity for more storage, but it's not easily accessed. Instead of a long row of uninterrupted and hard-to-reach upper cabinets, a collection of inexpensive clocks, purchased from museum stores, adds the visual interest we needed in this monochromatic kitchen.

An important decision in every project is what to hang over a king-size bed. We usually look for a large horizontal piece of art or a group of small pieces that we can hang in a grid. When we saw this piece of sculpture at an art show, we knew immediately that it was ideal for this energetic and art-loving young family.

LEFT: The color scheme in the master bath is limited to shades of white, cream, and silver except for the celestial blue ceiling. OPPOSITE: One of the client's favorite spots is her reading room, where she can relax in her Bibliochaise from Nobody and Co. The theme of transparency reappears in the art-glass pieces we commissioned for the bookshelves.

Don't be afraid of a pattern on a large sofa. More forgiving to stains than a solid, pattern becomes more subdued on a larger piece. In the upstairs family room, the carbon-fiber desk chair is a nod to the owner's love of racecars. Fur-covered stools turn the coffee table into a child-size game table.

78

OPPOSITE: In this ideal configuration, the upstairs family room opens to the playroom, where plain white walls are enhanced with cubbies and cabinets color blocked in the owner's favorite shades of raspberry, blue, purple, and yellow. RIGHT: A hand-painted stencil of tire tracks runs up a wall in the little boy's bedroom.

Instead of wallpaper, we stenciled all the children's rooms, because paint is easy to change, and it's easy enough to fix accidental doodles and marks. Every room, even in a sundrenched house like this, has layered lighting including playful chandeliers like these two in the girls' rooms.

PRECEDING PAGES: In the dining area outside, a tropical-blue Prouvé-inspired table and lacy chairs are just right for poolside entertaining. RIGHT: Indoor-outdoor rugs have come so far in the decorating galaxy. We used this one to unify the floor plan of a massive L-shape sofa and a pair of chaise pods in the seating area. The groups of pillows repeat the palette of the house.

86

A NEW LOOK

nterior design is never static. While designers often boast that their designs are timeless, the truth is that we are all influenced by the trends and changes that surround us. We wouldn't be scouring books, magazines, and blogs if we weren't.

These clients asked us to reimagine their classic apartment and help them achieve a new, more modern look. We had previously decorated this apartment, but they felt it was time for an update. They wanted to keep most of their beautiful antique furniture, and they especially did not want to undertake any physical renovation of the spaces. No one with four children and three dogs wants to relocate while the decorators make decisions about moldings and paint.

It's difficult to part with the things you love, and you shouldn't if they are meaningful to you. This is a common struggle for clients who decide to redesign a space. They want to refresh, but they rarely want to see their favorite pieces disappear. As much as we try, it's usually impossible to truly rejuvenate a space by simply moving around existing furniture. But we love a challenge, so we went to work.

We started with an easy fix, reupholstering sofas and chairs by switching out multi-colored taffetas and damask weaves for simpler, monochromatic textures. Multi-colored chintzes, curvilinear and floral patterns, and designs with realistic imagery tend to evoke a traditional feel. One-color woven fabrics and those with unusual textures feel more modern because they are usually used to highlight the simplicity of modern forms. The new fabrics and trim were also chosen with an eye toward adding some spark and new glamour with metallic and iridescent threads. The clients were so delighted with the results that they asked for more. It quickly became apparent that a simple revision would not be enough to achieve the full effect that they wanted.

In the expanded scope, all the walls, ceilings, and trim were repainted. We have always been partial to glazes rather than flat paint because in a glaze, the paint particles are suspended in a translucent medium, which allows the light to shimmer over the surface. This is not necessarily modern, but here the glazes are often high

OPPOSITE: Because hallways are transitional spaces, we often use a neutral palette to help the connecting rooms flow seamlessly. Contrary to intuition, a runner makes a narrow space feel wider than traditional wall-to-wall carpet. The red bench and the blue LED artwork punctuate the end of the long hall. OVERLEAF: In the entry, the ebonized furniture is echoed in the black marble cabochon in the ochre-and-white marble floor. The arrangement of objects on the entrance hall console foreshadows the whimsical spirit of the apartment.

gloss or over-washed with a metallic finish, which, together with a lighter palette, infused the apartment with a feeling of sleek modernity.

Continuing the quest to make everything new and brighter, we then addressed the lighting and light fixtures. Larger lamps, brighter bulbs, and simpler shades can really change an environment. With wood or ceramic forms, bigger, more sculptural lamps feel less traditional than small ones. Intriguing materials like metal, glass, and crystal also reflect the light and add interest. Swap out dark smocked or pleated shades for simple white or ecru paper and linen. Take the little shades off the chandelier arms and change the bulbs to frosted flame tip or clear torpedo shapes. In this apartment, new recessed art lights replaced the wall-mounted picture lights to add a more gallery-like feeling.

S till, the furniture plan is classic and the rooms are all well proportioned and arranged. The living room has sofas and chairs in conversation groups, tables and lamps where needed for a drink. The library is filled with well-read books and personal collections, and the dining room is both livable enough for family dinners and stylish enough for holiday gatherings. The glamour of the final effect mirrors the clients' personality and style. It's a comfortable opulence that's easy to live with.

RIGHT: In this mix of traditional and modern, the ornate curves of the Louis XV–style mantel with its amber-colored Bresciato marble and the flanking pair of gilded Biedermeier consoles are balanced by the square-armed sofa and the custom-designed wood-framed modernist chairs. Selecting what to hang on either side of a mantel is a critical decision. Of all the options, one piece of art and two mirrors is our favorite because the mirrors bring reflected light where there usually is none, and finding two mirrors is easier than finding two pieces of art that coordinate. OVERLEAF: In the refresh of the apartment, the over-scale Empire chandelier, the Regency sofa table, and the Biedermeier center table—all beloved antiques—were retained.

A view of the enfilade of the library, living, and dining room. One important consideration where rooms open onto each other is the balance of tones and color. On the near side of the honey-stained-pine paneled library, the living room walls are finished in venetian stucco with an outline of an ashlar stone pattern. At the far end, the dining room is finished with bark paper applied in a running-bond brick pattern.

In the library, the backs
of the bookcases are
covered in golden
pearl-coated paper that
softly reflects light.
As always, bookcase
harmony is essential
and is achieved with a mix
of open and closed
arrangements, including
books and objects of
different shapes and
materials. The sculpture
in front of the window
is by Eric Fischl.

98

In the dining room,
diamond patterned sisal
carpet offsets the
traditional feeling of the
table, chairs and the
red-lacquer Leleu
sideboard. We ebonized
the client's set of chairs,
added a gold outline,
and upholstered them in
silver faux shagreen.
The gold leaf ceiling
contrasts with the silver
leaf in the living room.

His and hers studies. The daybed in her study is upholstered with an over-scale abstract zebra print. Making a daybed with a pretty cover like this one lets you enjoy the luxury of lounging when guests aren't around. A lacquered cinnabar-red mirror frame enhances his paneled study.

PRECEDING PAGES, LEFT AND RIGHT: A master bedroom is a great place to indulge in silk fabrics, carpet, and other delicate finishes because it doesn't get a tremendous amount of wear and tear. These walls are upholstered in a pale cream ottoman silk and finished with bronze nail heads. The bronze tones are repeated in the metallic threads of the Lessage embroidered cuffs on the silk curtains, and the nail heads are repeated on the gold leather chairs. The headboard and bed legs are mirrored, adding a note of glamour.

A reinterpretation of a 1950s Palm Beach palette of turquoise, orange, and yellow creates one of our favorite schemes for the teenage daughter's bedroom. Details like the Hermes vintage scarf repurposed as a pillow personalize the room of this young equestrian.

Hollywood glam is the message for another daughter. Elements like the silver leather tub chair overlay a classic bedroom that can easily be redecorated as a guest room in years to come.

LEFT: For the youngest child, painted stripes are an homage to his favorite sports team. A child's room is the ideal place to be bold with color. OPPOSITE: We updated the kitchen without redoing any cabinetry. We glazed the ceiling Tiffany blue, added a back-painted glass table top on the existing table base to match, and switched out bistro chairs for these wrapped in washable white leather.

POSH PIED-À-TERRE

Many empty nesters dream of leaving the suburbs and finding a glamorous pied-à-terre in the center of the city. For longstanding clients of ours, this two-bedroom apartment, in a gracious prewar building by the famed architect Rosario Candela, was just that kind of apartment. Still keeping their family house in Connecticut, they found a new lifestyle in Manhattan, perfect for their weekdays in the city.

The owners didn't need a big kitchen or a space for entertaining; they had that in the suburbs. What they wanted was a younger, fresher interior—a mix of traditional and more modern furniture, artwork that would definitely skew to abstraction, and an exciting and vibrant palette. Working with architect John B. Murray, we gutted the apartment and renovated every inch to make everything up-to-date, fresh, and clean.

We started with the living room floor plan, since this is the main room of the apartment. The typical setting would have the two sofas and a coffee table flanking the fireplace and perhaps a small dining table near the opening from the gallery. By splitting the seating on the diagonal and moving the table to the window, we accomplished so much. Instead of a sofa with its back to the windows at the corner of the room, the small dining table takes advantage of the classic city view. Separating the large upholstered pieces and including a dining area also makes the room feel much bigger.

The L-shape sofa is a modern touch, while a vintage piece—an irresistibly shaped sofa from the Marché aux Puces in Paris—is a foil to the more traditional architecture and adds a note of whimsy to the room. On the other hand, the clean lines of the classically inspired brass-and-glass coffee tables blend seamlessly into the interior. The related yet different designs of all these elements give the living room texture and interest.

Mixing beloved antiques with a new palette and a few contemporary pieces is one of the best ways to make traditional look modern. Design today is not an all-or-nothing proposition. For example, we now use a

OPPOSITE: The entry walls are venetian stucco painted with a sinuous sgraffito line of gold to soften the architecture and the symmetrical furniture arrangement. An intensely painted ceiling like this one in peacock blue raises the line of sight and makes the ceiling feel higher. OVERLEAF: Staggered seating areas open up the room. Curtains in ribbed aqua silk with bronze embroidery reinforce the entry ceiling color, uniting the two spaces in the small apartment.

wider variety of upholstery forms than previously because being "less strict" about the shapes adds a more eclectic vibe, which feels right in today's world. From antique shops to auction houses to couture, a broad range of sources can generate an equally broad range of styles.

This client brought her adventurous eye and great zeal to the project, and we were very inspired by her desire for unexpected color combinations, which we expressed in the palette of the paint colors, the fabrics, and the hard materials. In a sunlit space like this, it's fun to celebrate saturated color. The palette we used when we first started our business was drawn from Chinese porcelain and antique carpets. Indigo, hunter, cinnabar, ochre, and aubergine were the dominant colors. Here the carpet is a new silk leopard-like spotted rug in neutral shades of tan and brown. Instead of indigo, we used aqua and marine blue for the curtains and upholstery. Aubergine is translated into sleek mauve in the master bedroom, and ochre has morphed into citrine in the office/guest room.

Incorporating contemporary ideas and a fresh palette, the new apartment is a perfect balance of past and present, brimming with personality and character.

We love coffee table harmony. In this room, the tables are brass, similar yet subtly different. The two shown here have shelves and ball finials while a third, without a shelf, is brass and lucite. Part of updating traditional décor is the freedom to combine shades of one color. Mixing shades of peacock, Persian, aqua, and royal blue feels more dynamic than a carefully measured palette.

The master bedroom is luxuriously wrapped in a hand-painted De Gornay paper with silver accents that brighten the mauve background. It was fun to play on this palette with the claret color of the glass in the lamp, the chandelier, and in the lavender threads in the bedding embroidery details. White woodwork and linens ensure the saturated walls don't dominate.

We celebrate color in the sunlit guest room/study with saturated citrine walls and accents. Styling a daybed with pillows, as we did here, makes it look more like a sofa than a guest bed. Because the room multitasks, the apartment feels larger than it would if this second bedroom were simply a guest room.

SOUTHERN HOSPITALITY

I t is enormously satisfying to be involved in a collaborative project, especially when your partners are the best in their field. This was the case when our sophisticated clients in Houston brought together Allan Greenberg as the architect, Deborah Nevins as the landscape designer, and our team to design their new home. Connecting not just with the client but also with other professionals from the very beginning is like a dream. Not only can we fine tune our decorating decisions at every step, but seeing a project from inception to completion is a luxury that we never take for granted because, in our experience, true collaboration always leads to the best results.

A great advantage to starting from scratch is the freedom to explore. Right from the start, we knew that this family wanted bedrooms for their grown children, guest rooms, and some quiet space for the family, as well as more formal interiors and gardens to entertain guests both inside and out. Allan Greenberg's brilliant design, with multiple north–south and east–west axes, highlights both the dramatic vistas from room to room and from all rooms to the exterior. The 13-foot ceilings reinforce this connection with the gardens, as triple-hung windows and multiple French doors open to terraces surrounding the building on all sides. Deborah Nevins's dynamic landscape, including a magnificent azalea garden, provides a focal point at all elevations.

One of the most important considerations in design, always, is a sense of place. Since this is their primary residence, our clients wanted their home to reflect the city's historic heritage as well as its location in the South. It's a very grand and proper house, but it's also airy, light, and cheerful, with light colors and materials that respond to heat and sunshine. This was very important: they wanted to walk in and feel cool relief from the Houston climate. We accomplished that by keeping the palette to a range of white, off-white,

In the entry, Picasso ceramics and a Richard Serra drawing contrast with the more traditional
forms of the Regency center table and credenza, the Biedermeier chairs, and the Empire chandelier.
The painted white stucco walls bring a welcome sense of refuge from the Southern heat.

and refreshing sherbet tones of color. The minimal palette also helps maintain a good balance between the more formal architectural elements, the gardens, and the sculptural furniture and modern art.

The clients' burgeoning collection of modern and contemporary art had a tremendous impact on the floor plan. Typically, contemporary art requires what we call a "floating" furniture plan because the canvases are too large to hang above a sofa or a console table. With the extremely high ceilings in this residence, however, we were able to put many important works of art above sofas, mantels, and sideboards. The ability to put furniture against a wall adds a traditional feeling to our design.

To reinforce this juxtaposition of the traditional and the modern, we mixed custom-made pieces with a range of nineteenth- and early twentieth-century English, Continental, and American furniture and objects. The pieces chosen are more straight-lined than curvy, and imposing in size, scale, and purpose. Their linear quality keeps the interiors feeling up-to-date and not the least bit stuffy, and we were faithful to that standard. If an object had too much ormolu and elaborate inlay and lacked a strong silhouette, it didn't pass muster.

All of the broad strokes and all of the details here—from inside to out, from floor plans to fabrics—are the result of the fully collaborative spirit employed from day one on this project, and which all add up to an extraordinary new home.

The reception hall to the left of the entry adds an extra path of circulation. The massive table was bought at auction at a surprisingly good price because of its hard-to-place scale. In spaces like this where the decorating is subordinate to the architecture, using a single commanding piece is enough of a statement.

The living room is organized into three seating areas. At one end, a painting by Hans Hoffman hangs over a mantel designed by Jamb in London with inlaid chocolate-brown emperador stone. The Empire chandelier is one of a pair in the room and the twentieth-century bronze sconces are from a set of four.

The considerations of a warm climate, a light palette, and traditional furnishings drove an exhaustive search for antique rugs that weren't in the usual palette of saturated colors. We were pleased to find this pale-blue, chocolate-brown, and beige Tabriz for the living room. The warm tones of the dusty-rose accent pillows relate to the peach tones of the dining room across the hall. To keep color flowing between rooms, we try to introduce the dominant palette of one space into the accents of another.

OPPOSITE: The octagonal apse at the garden end of the living room is the spot for afternoon tea. Because we prefer not to use shaped rugs, the space is defined instead by a strongly patterned specimen marble tabletop and an unusual set of Biedermeier chairs. Curtains are trimmed with appliqued and embroidered panels. RIGHT: The powder room sink was fashioned out of an antique chest retrofitted with plumbing fixtures and an onyx top. In a twist on a classic design, we recolored a Chinese wallpaper in a new palette of cool silver and warm beige.

The formal dining room shimmers
with rose-gold glazed walls, a
nineteenth-century empire ormolu
and cut-glass chandelier, and a
Richard Pousette-Dart painting.
Eliminating sconces over the
fireplace created space for the large
work by Lee Krasner.

The wood paneling in the library was simply sealed to keep the color
light and to maintain the visual interest of the wood grain.
The cabinet under the Hans Hoffman works brilliantly by allowing
the painting to carefully slide down and the television to pop up.

Holophane pendant lights are placed within the elaborate honeycomb pattern of the ceiling moldings. Suspended fixtures illuminate the ceiling and especially the people in a room in a far more flattering way than down lights. At the far end, the octagonal apse of the breakfast room matches that in the living room. Kitchen seating areas like this one are a good place to flesh out details with soft curtains and a more decorative light fixture like this three-tiered chandelier.

139

Alan Greenberg punctuated the bedroom hall with a circular space defined by an overhead cupola that brings in daylight. The compass rose inlaid on the floor enhances the drama of the rotunda as there are no soft furnishings to provide pattern or decorative detail.

Because antique beds
are never wider than
sixty inches, we
custom made this
mahogany king-size
bed in an antique
manner with gilded
accents. Metalwork,
like that on the
bedside tables, and
stone tops, like the
one on the dresser,
also help break up the
uniformity of wood.

These are the most glamorous his-and-hers bathrooms we have ever been privileged to work on. The white stone grid unites the bathrooms, while the accent stone changes from her blue celeste to his green onyx. His jade-colored stone is a luxurious foil to the rich, dark wood of the paneling and the dresser.

ROOMS WITH A VIEW

I love the way people come to us so sure of how their future home will look. There are so many shelter magazines and design blogs that give great access to visual inspiration, and many new clients seem to know exactly what they want. But decorating is a lot like falling in love: you can daydream all you want, but you may fall in love with what you least expect. And you may have to trust us to lead you there.

In this case, the owner professed to want an uber-traditional place in Manhattan with rich, dark paneling, multicolored rugs, and clubby antiques. But then we took him shopping, and he literally had a *coup de foudre* over an Art Deco cabinet by Maxime Old that now sits in the entry, setting the stage for the interiors to come. Much more contemporary than he and his wife had originally expected, the piece suggested a completely new direction, and it was a very exciting departure for us, too.

Before we could begin to decorate, John B. Murray presented an innovative architectural solution to combine two adjacent apartments on the tenth floor of a landmarked building designed by Schwartz & Gross in 1925. More than space planning, he came up with an architectural vocabulary to define the completely re-done aerie that reflected the owners' new-found love for Art Deco and Hollywood Regency. With more than sixty-five feet of majestic views overlooking Central Park framed by the city skyline, the new space was exactly what they wanted since they intended to host friends and family throughout the year.

This desire to entertain drove the apartment layout toward an open floor plan with a big welcoming kitchen, more like a large new house than a traditional apartment. John Murray had the brilliant idea of putting the kitchen, with enough space for a large breakfast table, at the front of the apartment, directly off the entry. The new configuration of kitchen/dining room allows for park views from the kitchen, where everyone congregates to cook and party. The surprise of a kitchen in the front of an apartment in a historic prewar building on Fifth Avenue gave us the freedom to break from tradition and create a less formal design scheme.

The library view extends over Central Park to the towers of the San Remo.
To frame the vista, curtain panels are installed with fabric stacked
outside the window frame, leaving almost the full width of the glass open.

RIGHT: The entry is the center of circulation. Instead
of a rug, the dramatic marble floor adds pattern. The circular
shape of the plaster medallion in the ceiling is repeated
in the brass metal work of the Italian chandelier from
the 1940s and again in the custom mahogany center table.
OVERLEAF: In the living room, an expansive space with a
relatively low ceiling height, it was challenging to find
a chandelier with enough mass to hold its own. The 1960s
Italian chandelier is a perfect solution. Its irregular shape
reads like a piece of sculpture, and the glass rods
hanging from the brass armature lighten its visual load.

Every room now takes advantage of the view with some kind of seating. In the dining room, a section of the large table seating eighteen can stand alone in front of the window for more intimate dinners. In the living room, club chairs overlook the view with a small table for a drink in the evening or morning coffee and the paper. In the library, there's a partner's desk for catching up on work or looking out at the skyline, and in the master bedroom, the quintessential chaise is ready for reading or contemplative appreciation.

The opportunity to work with the clients' art collection added a special dimension to the project. In an era where the art market is obsessed with abstraction, the focus here on representational art is surprisingly refreshing. In a more traditionally decorated apartment, representational art would look expected, but here it adds a new point of view. The collection explores figuration in its many modes—landscapes and seascapes, the human figure, and interior scenes. Spanning the late nineteenth century to the present, the pieces range from American modern masters such as Childe Hassam and Stuart Davis to contemporary emerging artist Cynthia Knott. The art steered many of our choices about finishes and fabrics, leading us towards richly understated tonal materials so as not to overpower the art or the exquisitely detailed architectural envelope.

RIGHT AND OVERLEAF: In the living room, a painting by William Trost Richards, a nineteenth-century landscape artist, in its original frame is a highlight of the apartment. Bursts of russet on the pillows and on the top of the coffee table complement the warm wood tones to brighten the prevailing creamy taupe palette. The silk area rug has a modernized Chinese fretwork design. The mantel was custom made by Jamb in London.

LEFT: The enfilade of the dining room, living room, library, and master bedroom is lit by the windows facing Fifth Avenue. OPPOSITE: The metal end tables and the black-lacquer coffee table contrast with the paneling of the library. OVERLEAF: The dining room is designed for flexibility in seating. The three-pedestal table divides so that one pedestal can be moved to the window, taking advantage of the view for intimate dinners of two or four.

PRECEDING PAGES: The
spacious eat-in family
kitchen opens directly off
of the glamorous entry.
OPPOSITE: The master
bedroom is an oasis of
calm with pale lavender
venetian stucco walls.
At the window, the
sensuously curved tufted
back chaise has a
fruitwood frame that
augments its sculptural
quality. RIGHT: Serenely
refined untrimmed
curtains in an overall
pattern hang from narrow
bronze rings and rods
that do not compete with
the architectural detail.

CONTEMPORARY CLASSIC

I t's easy to fall in love with a fabulous historic property—especially if it's Holly Hill, the one-hundred-year-old house once owned by Brooke Astor. Set on more than sixty acres of land overlooking the Hudson River, this beautifully proportioned, light-filled house is surrounded by magnificent trees, formal gardens, and outdoor entertaining areas. Our clients were smitten, but the challenge was figuring out how to breathe new life into the interior spaces without wiping the slate clean.

The first task was to bring the house into the twenty-first century. Architect Oscar Shamamian added a new wing with a mudroom, a connecting family room with comfortable sofas, and a large eat-in kitchen. This new multi-purpose space, which would never have existed in the 1920s, is integral to the bustling suburban life this family leads.

The next step was to transform the traditional Delano & Aldrich design into a plan for modern living while honoring the history and preserving many of the original architectural details. Renovating and restoring rather than replacing the original plaster moldings, fireplace mantels, and the sweeping stair and railing in the entry ensured that the house maintained its traditional shell and formality. The house's pedigree demanded brass hardware for the doors and windows, but the owners preferred a silver-colored finish for all the new elements. The mixed metals lend a welcome and informal feeling to the classic spaces.

In the past, we might have filled a house like this with antique rugs and furniture, intricate curtains, and representational art. Instead the clients asked for a more casual feeling and for an upbeat sensibility to allow their two teenage children to be comfortable throughout.

The original marble floor and graceful foliate design of the Delano & Aldrich railing
were left untouched in the renovation. The cool gray wall color, abstract paintings up
the steps, and the streamlined Jansen table give the space an airy feeling.

As is true with all projects, form follows function in every room. This meant that the enormous living room, for example, which must have hosted parties for one hundred in its heyday, was reimagined as a multi-purpose room. We included an area for television and an L-shaped sofa, a sitting area with a chaise overlooking the grounds, and, in between, a new pool table below an Art Deco—inspired billiards light. To unite the areas and warm the room, we designed an 18-by-35-foot rug. The newly woven, loose loop Berber carpet has an informal style, making the room more inviting, while its design pays homage to the geometry of the original parquet de Versailles flooring in all the principal rooms.

We used a palette of cool grays—the owner's favorite color is Dior gray—the walls throughout are painted in subtly different shades. Still, each room has its own complementary color, seen in light accents within the upholstery fabrics, a cashmere blanket, or even a large-scale work of art. In the living room, we played with tones of burgundy, in the library, shades of blue. In the dining room a red-lacquer sideboard references the oxblood red of the original stone mantels.

Holly Hill was the place where Brooke Astor loved to relax. She once compared her time here to "backing up to the Esso and getting refueled." Today, her country home is once again serving as a retreat, but this time for an active family building new memories in a home we hope she would approve.

OPPOSITE AND OVERLEAF: In a traditional house like this, the art collection would be framed, easel-sized paintings or works on paper hung within the boundaries of the moldings. Instead, we hung the art, an extensive collection of large-scale contemporary photography, right over the moldings.

The more formal side of the living room overlooks the rear terrace and the dramatic view of the Hudson. Bordeaux-colored velvet on the chaise enhances the elegant mood set by the cream, gray, and black palette. Square mirrored legs on the sofa and conical gilded ones on the chaise contrast with the informality of the room-sized Berber rug.

In the library, twelve-foot ceilings and arched windows were a challenge. With windows so close together and so tall, we used an all-over patterned fabric instead of a solid with a decorative edge, which would have been too linear in this room. Like the artwork, we hung the curtain rods right over the moldings and the keystones, preserving these details but not being intimidated by them. In a happy coincidence, the concentric circles in the photograph echo the overhead lights and the arched doors and windows.

A dining chair with a wood back has a lot of interest but not a lot of comfort. Upholstered backs with a clever detail like this brass pull on the top of the frame is the best of both worlds. The custom three-pedestal table is walnut, the carpet is go-with-everything casual sisal, and the chandelier is late twentieth-century Venini style with smoked Murano glass panels.

In the new wing, a combination kitchen and family room responds to
the needs of a busy family. The white kitchen is seasoned with a natural
wood island, and the warm wood color is echoed in the coffee table.

The sweeping design of the new porch allows for panoramic views of the property and its spectacular holly trees. We mixed light and dark materials to keep an animated feeling in the open space. The coffee table and the armillary are both wrought iron, the sofa bases are ebonized wood, and the four bone lamps sit on custom side tables of bleached walnut.

The pool area is reminiscent of the Hollywood Regency style of the 1920s and 1930s. Every outdoor area should be furnished with as much attention to detail as an indoor one. Here we accessorized with pillows and a striped awning that are typical of the great selection of outdoor fabrics on the market today.

"SOME LIKE IT HOT"

I adore theater and movies, and I have the good fortune of having two sons "in the business." I simply love the immersive feeling of how a good set, stage, or movie can transport you. That creative fantasy is what inspires me to participate in decorator show houses, allowing me to create a storyline, design a set, and execute my vision. Like a movie, show houses require an enormous amount of collaboration. Colleagues in our office, artisans, vendors, and show house volunteers all rally to push and pull ideas around until the very last minute. Show house design is always an aerobic test, since we typically have just six weeks to achieve our vision. But it's always a lot of fun for a very good cause.

For the 42nd Kip's Bay Decorator Show House, we decided to design the bedroom as an homage to the iconic movie *Some Like It Hot* and create a warm, sexy environment within the grand Villard Houses on Madison Avenue.

The room was huge, and the first consideration had to be the floor plan, which was delineated by a wall of windows and a fireplace. The furniture arrangement came together easily with the bed opposite the fireplace and a cozy seating arrangement in front. If the room were smaller and we had no choice, the bed could be closer to the fireplace, but this was the optimal arrangement for this room.

In a very large room that accommodates two seating areas, we always prefer a single rug to unite the space. Additionally, one rug prevents an awkward empty space between the two areas, and eliminates the unwelcome possibility of two different types and sizes of rugs in one room. We try to start the design of every room with the rug because so many factors come into play in finding the right one. In this case, it was especially important to start there because we needed a rug in the right size, and we knew that would be a challenge.

We fell in love with the design of this carpet, a Beauvais reproduction based on a Louis XIV rug from Hubert de Givenchy's house in Paris. It was especially fortuitous because the size was so perfect that it gave us our ideal border of 12 to 18 inches between the rug and the walls. The best parts were the glam-

OPPOSITE: The room is filled with lush details, such as gold-leaf walls, a 1940s-inspired blue-lacquered bed, an exotic palm-frond table, a custom gold sateen bed cover, embroidered linens, and a fur throw. The faceted mirror by Claudia Weisser adds a cubist view of the room. OVERLEAF: It's easy to see how the rug connects the two areas and how the cobalt-blue accent for the room originated in the border.

orous overall pattern and rich colors. The palette reminded all of us of the rose gold bangle bracelet that I wear almost every day, and this seemed like a good sign. Without a client to filter your decisions, a good sign is a good thing!

If you allow the rug's color and style to inspire your decisions, the path to designing the whole room becomes clearer. The palette, the fabric choices, and the furniture styles can all flow from the statement the rug makes. Even the size of the rug can help with your decisions. In this case, knowing there would be two seating areas but one large rug convinced us that one chandelier would work best to unite the two areas.

Having the rug decided, the chandelier placed, and the decision about the bed and the seating area solidified, we were in good shape. But at this early stage of planning, we always take into account that a floor plan is more than just shapes on the floor; we consider materials and color at the very beginning to ensure a good variety of forms and interesting styles.

From the outset, our goal was for a dynamic mix of antique furniture that would represent our modern traditional design philosophy and convey the sophisticated and sensual feeling we hoped to create in the room. Ultimately, a dramatic French 1940s–inspired four-poster bed, an exotic gilt-bronze and rosewood marquetry cabinet with inlaid figures, and Art Deco consoles in ash burl with patinated bronze details were used as the "main events" to set the stage. Of particular note are a pair of cut-glass night tables with gilded beads and an overscaled, hand-blown and molded Murano glass chandelier from the 1950s.

We decided to pull out the blue tones from the rug as an accent color to complement the abundance of warm tones in the room, especially the rose-gold leafed walls. But rather than sprinkle the color around the room, we limited the blue to the vibrant glass behind the Regency brass grilles on the closet doors flanking the fireplace and to the cobalt lacquer of the bed. Adding more blue, to the upholstery for example, would have diluted its impact. Book ending the room with the accent color also helps unite the two sides of the room.

Thousands of people walk through the Kips Bay Show House and others like it all over the country. Our hope was to transport them with our sexy—but G-rated—room. With a new perspective and some new ideas about design, we tried to bring in the same immersive experience we all enjoy at the theater.

With all the "hot" colors in the room, cream-colored silk on the period Jansen chairs adds cool relief. Even the colored balls of candy in the glass bowl match the palette.

LEFT: A photograph by
Lisa Kereszi literally
expresses our theme of
"Some Like It Hot." Ivory
allegorical figures adorn
the panels of a bow-front-
ed rosewood cabinet from
1938. RIGHT: We are
always looking for ways to
animate non-working
fireplaces, and these brass
obelisks do the trick.

188

OCEANFRONT SOPHISTICATION

Who doesn't dream of a vacation house on the beach, one that's casual yet sophisticated and modern? This shingle style house in the Hamptons was designed for a family we've been working with for many years. Alongside architect Tom Kligerman and landscape architect Edmund Hollander, we brought their latest passion project to reality.

What sets the house apart is the razor-sharp attention to every aspect of the design and the balance between all of the hard and soft elements. Nothing is a given or a throw-away or an after-thought. Inside the gracefully weathering shingled exterior, there are modern architectural elements like the staircase, which incorporates an elegant metal railing, a spare, elemental take on a classic Greek meander, and massive hand-scraped white-oak timber treads. Wide-plank rough-hewn floors anchor the high style of horizontally inlaid, bronze-banded polished plaster walls and boarded wooden ceilings.

We are always looking to update traditional elements and integrating our ideas into this architecture felt very clean, couture, and of-the-moment. Every piece of furniture is either vintage or thoughtfully designed using exceptional materials, including natural wood, glass, metals, and metallic finishes. Forms are geometric and very tailored in keeping with the overall feeling of luxurious modern simplicity.

The innovation here is that the upholstery details, while custom, are never conspicuous. The wood-framed living room sofas are neatly upholstered in white with rolled self-welts instead of contrasting trim. The living room curtains are edged with an original hand-embroidered modern graphic, but the pattern is subtly colored and the fabric is understated off-white linen. While the idea of treating the fronts and leading edges of your curtains may not be new, using goatskin embroidery on humble white linen certainly is.

OPPOSITE: Entries are small but important spaces, and every element must be carefully considered. Here, the Gunther Forg painting with its dabs of vibrant color animates the beach palette of sand and stone. OVERLEAF: In the predominantly white living room, the art is the star attraction. The reflective surfaces on the Teresita Fernandez panels on the right are echoed in the metallic tables. In front of the fireplace is a fragmented table by contemporary London-based craftsmen and in the foreground, a vintage Philip Hiquily table from the 1970s.

There is no better inspiration than the colors of the sky, the water, and the beach so we let nature take the lead and allowed the vistas to drive the palette. We blended white and cream with the wood tones and metallic finishes and let the beautifully sculpted gardens and the art fill the rooms with color. Mostly white walls and materials also set off the art collection in the best way. It's almost like a gallery, but in a far softer and more personal way.

It is fascinating to see how an art collection can evolve as tastes change. Years ago, these clients collected American art and folk art for their home in Boston. Then they focused on midcentury American art for their pied-à-terre in Manhattan, and now they have moved forward in time and place in this new house, where the collection explores abstraction from World War II to the present. This home is a worthy partner to summer vacations in the Hamptons, to an excellent collaboration of professionals and clients, and, especially, to the art.

OPPOSITE: The inlaid bronze bands of the entry walls are repeated in the crown molding in the living room. The contemporary glass lamp has a circular design that echoes the round mirrored panel covered in bindi dots by Bharti Kher.
OVERLEAF: The dining room features a custom C&K table with an eglomisé top, an ethereal chandelier fashioned from dried dandelions, and a set of French 1940s sycamore chairs attributed to André Arbus, upholstered in faux suede.

In the library, the back
cushions of the sofa are
defined by quilted
concentric squares.
Goatskin embroidered
curtain panels hang
from bronze poles.
The highlight of the room
is the Ruhlman panel
nestled in the bookcase,
which is said to be one
of two surviving
from the *Normandie*.

The white glass kitchen cabinets are edged in oak. The island lights are originally from a theater in Stockholm, but we found them at the Marché aux Puces in Paris. The stainless-steel appliances add an open feeling to the orderly space and reflect the beautiful light from the beach just outside the windows.

The commanding view
of the ocean dominates
the master bedroom.
The modern sculptural
bed and the straw
marquetry side tables are
custom C&K designs.
There is an understated
feeling of serenity
created by the textures
of the silk carpet, the
woven bed throw, and
the boarded ceiling, but
it would feel flat without
the pops of the marine-
blue lamps and vases.
The pale-blue armchair
is one of a pair by
Robsjohn-Gibbings.

A study alcove overlooking the ocean is combined with the dressing room. Because modern design usually employs flat panels, it was important to us to articulate the woodwork with metal edges and hardware. The faces of the closet doors are upholstered with woven silver panels and the contemporary pulls and hinges are square.

The freestanding shower in the master
bath is like an outside shower. Mechanized
window shades come up from the floor to
allow privacy and light at the same time.

When working with tonal interiors and very strong light at the beach, it's important to incorporate texture, and it doesn't have to be subtle. In the guestroom, sheer curtains have an inset panel of contrast fabric strategically placed at eye level, and the natural linen headboard is defined by a horizontal band of three-dimensional embroidery.

RIGHT: We often change wall treatments on a bed wall. In the son's room, the back wall is boarded in whitewashed oak, repeating the material from the passageway doors in the house. OVERLEAF: The pool has a commanding view of the dunes and the Atlantic Ocean.

210

OUTSIDER ART AT HOME

As designers, one of the most exciting journeys we take is working with an art collection that is unfamiliar to us. In this Central Park West apartment, we had the great fortune to work with a very important collection of outsider art. Created by untrained artists who work outside of the mainstream art world, often living outside the boundaries of conventional society, this work sits at the intersection of modern art and folk art. Many of the sculptures and paintings here are very colorful and made with atypical materials, all of which make a collection like this very dynamic to live with.

Two aspects of this project were unique. First, we rarely see a comprehensive collection like this in a home. And second, the owner is my beloved nephew. A common fear about working with friends and family is that you shouldn't mix business with pleasure. As a designer, I absolutely feel the opposite way—I love working with people with whom I am close. Working together makes our relationships even stronger, and the extra time we spend together shopping for antiques, analyzing paint colors, test driving upholstery forms and the like is always so much fun. In fact, the decorator/client relationship is so intense that just about every client has now become a personal friend.

My nephew came to us not just because we are related, but also because he realized his apartment was basically an undecorated "bachelor pad" with a treadmill in the living room. In addition, the haphazardly placed art had begun to overwhelm the rambling prewar rooms, and the decor was no longer commensurate with the quality of the art. The main concern was to create a more sophisticated environment for his family and one that would be a worthy backdrop for the art. Like any great collector, he loves being able to add pieces and re-arrange the works, and he collects them not just because they are important, but also because he enjoys the personal discovery. But what we needed here was to find a new equilibrium between the art and the decorating.

OPPOSITE: The pair of table-top convex mirrors on the living room cabinet act like a piece of pop art. OVERLEAF: Over the years, we have typically used white for painted trim such as wall and window moldings. But since the walls are oyster colored here and there is very little decorative detail, the trim is painted in a darker color as a visual accent.

214

ATELIER INCURVE

AVEDON THE SIXTIES

We knew that the overall design, including the floor plan, furniture styles, palette, and the fabrics, would all have to accept an ever-changing arrangement of paintings, sculptures, and assemblages. We used mostly wooden, organic, and authentic hard materials without a lot of gloss. New upholstery shapes are tailored not ornate, and fabrics are mostly solid but still colorful enough to match the intensity of the highly patterned art without taking center stage.

In the living room, for example, the clean lines and sophisticated gray/beige mohair on a Jean Michel Frank–style sofa are just the right setting for the sculptural artworks hanging above. Throughout the apartment, we ordered standard curtain hardware and then made simple panels, just mixing up the recipe for each room. The living room curtains have a wide band of red contrast fabric across the bottoms, the library a cuff on the leading edge, and the dining room and master bedroom an embroidered fabric in an updated modern design to give them each a distinct personality.

Finding balance between the vivid art and the wall treatments was key to the success of the project, and we employed a variety of paint colors and finishes throughout the residence. The entry hall, which originally had a densely patterned wallpaper, now has clean white walls. New pieces can be hung right up without worrying about damaging decorative paint. But for drama and effect, we added a glossy taxicab-yellow on the ceiling. In the library, the deep tone of cornflower-blue high-gloss paint is an unexpected backdrop to the rich colors in the paintings. The hematite color painted below the chair rail in the dining room grounds the disparate colors of the vivid artwork.

The apartment's new design has a clean eclecticism with room for new ideas and discoveries. Now the interiors—organized, edited, and decorated—highlight the collection and allow the artwork to take a starring role.

OPPOSITE: A decorative firescreen sits in the living room fireplace. The flag over the mantel is made of paillets that reflect light in a play on what a typical mirror would have done.

OPPOSITE: Cornflower-blue walls in the library are an unexpected choice but serve as a cool balance to the energy of the art. The organic coffee table is by George Nakashima. ABOVE: The entry is hung with a rotating selection of pieces. OVERLEAF: The art in the dining room is an eclectic mix of drawings, a printing plate, paintings, and sculpture.

A SENSE OF PLACE

Right from the start we knew this project would be something special: a new oceanfront house in Palm Beach with panoramic views, designed in collaboration with architect Peter Zimmerman and landscape architect Jorge Sanchez. The owners, collectors of museum-quality American furniture and art, agreed that different styles, periods, and aesthetics should be brought in to give the house a world view. British-colonial tables, Murano glass mirrors, French beaded-glass pedestals, chinoiserie cabinets, and Russian chandeliers fill the rooms, while works of art from nineteenth-century masters such as Mary Cassatt and John Singer Sargent to twentieth-century icons such as Jackson Pollock and Willem de Kooning grace the walls. And to connect the disparate pieces, we drew our inspiration from the view of the ocean that greets you from every window.

We brought that seaside feeling inside with a light and sophisticated touch wherever possible. The living room curtains, embroidered in India, boast a shell motif; the family dining room carpet has a panoply of sea creatures; the family entry was stenciled in a sea turtle design; the kitchen backsplash is etched in a Lalique-inspired underwater tableau. But the most animated references to the shore are the grotto and the powder room, where the walls are encrusted with shells from all over the world.

A tropical palette was especially important to the DNA of the house. Shades of sunshine yellow, ocean blue, and vivid coral weave from room to room. Instead of pops of color, it's all about continuity of color, and there is always just enough in every room. Yellow flows from the plaster finished entry walls to the antique dining room wallpaper to the master bedroom's upholstered walls, embroidered curtains, and silk pillows.

Overlooking the ocean in Palm Beach, the house is filled with light, and every room has a spectacular view. Taking the tropical site as inspiration, the interiors honor the beachfront location in ways both classic and contemporary.

ABOVE AND RIGHT: The entry hall exemplifies the juxtaposition of old and new. By the front door are a Chinese Chippendale card table and Regency convex mirror. At the foot of the stairs, a painting by Roy Lichtenstein from the 1960s hangs above a George II marble top table by William Kent from 1740 and a rare pair of Chinese nodding head figures.

The sapphire-blue mirror in the entry leads to accents of blue in the library and the living room, the stone in the master bath, and to the guest rooms upstairs. From the glazed living room walls to the cozy upstairs sitting room, the whole house is brimming with warm shades of coral.

Every broad stroke of tradition has been reinterpreted with a new feeling of modernity. While in our more modern projects classic principles of design guide our process, here the lessons from modernism add a new and welcome tension to our more classical work. Although the rooms are filled with the finest quality antiques, these pieces are transformed by an edited envelope that adds clarity and cohesiveness. At the top of the stairs, under a silver leafed dome ceiling, the Chinese Chippendale balustrade meets a striking Hans Hoffman painting in the best way possible.

Like the other projects in the book, this home is all about the alchemy that happens when old meets new and when new meets old. Our strategy, always, is to have a fluid conversation between the cultures represented, the fine art and the furniture, and the overriding goals for function and comfort. We approach every project with the rigor of a jigsaw puzzle, but with the desire to create a magnificent tapestry.

We hope this book will set you on your own decorating journey full of the breadth and excitement of what's out there, and what you can discover to make into your own, regardless of your design vocabulary, from classic to contemporary.

From the entry portal the ocean beckons through the expansive living room windows. On the left is a sapphire-blue Venetian glass mirror over a mahogany, steel, and a Russian gilt-bronze cabinet from the late eighteenth century.

228

Like the prow of a ship, the windows encompass three exposures. A bay window can be a challenge, but roman shades like these speak to the windows, while the curtain in front respects the rectangular shape of the room. The twentieth-century art is a foil for the Regency oval center table, c. 1810, and the black-lacquer Chinese export chairs from 1735 at the window.

230

LEFT: One of a pair of George III Chinese soapstone-mounted padouk, rosewood, mahogany, and bamboo cabinets on stands, c. 1765. OPPOSITE: A vintage metal palm tree sculpture from the 1940s brings a sense of place and offsets the formality of the fine antiques, including the pair of Japanese Meiji-period gold and lacquer robe boxes on gilt-copper mounts used as coffee tables.

LEFT, RIGHT, AND PRECEDING PAGES: While the size and style of the house calls for a formal dining room, the space is open on the two long sides. On one side, a wall of French doors embraces loggias and flower filled gardens, and on the other, a colonnade of arches faces a corridor that opens to the sea. The traditional mood set by antique chinoiserie wallpaper from Williamsburg, a Duncan Phyfe pedestal table and a set of ten chairs attributed to the same maker is tempered by a silk flat-weave rug and crisp white moldings.

PRECEDING PAGES: In the library, a British colonial coffee table inlaid with a compass rose, tobacco jars, globes, and shell brackets suggest travel and the sea. ABOVE AND RIGHT: In the family entry and hall, a turtle stencil recalls the turtle migration so protected in Palm Beach. Off the entry, the pecky cypress construction of the ceiling mirrors the design of the limestone and oak floor. The wall of hanging orchids on the left is a signature of the house.

The white kitchen cabinets highlight the glass backsplash carved, in an homage to Lalique, with an elaborate seascape of underwater creatures.

The east loggia, facing the sea, is one of twelve. We brought the inside out with comfortable upholstered furniture. A rare eighteenth-century specimen marble top is mounted on an anodized-aluminum coffee table base.

Upstairs, a George I green-lacquer bookcase that was formerly in the Fogg Art Museum stands at the end of a hall. On the landing at the top of the stairs is a carved-mahogany Regency sofa with brass inlay and lion's paw feet from 1810. Lemon-yellow stucco walls and aluminum leaf in the shallow dome reflect the sunshine.

PRECEDING PAGES: In the master suite, the tailored simplicity of the ticking stripe upholstered bed and clean white sofa is offset by the crystal chandelier and lamps and by the embroidered floral curtain fabric.

OPPOSITE: Her dressing room is decorated with doors paneled in an eglomisé design of stylized fretwork and sea creatures, a chandelier from the 1960s and a Lalique mirror over a neoclassical chest.

RIGHT: His dressing room is paneled in honey-stained anigre. The fireplace surround is Tiffany glass.

In the dressing table niche of the master bath is a Tiffany window with a Rhulmann vanity and chair from 1925. The wood furniture adds warmth to the bathroom, and the luster ware in the shelves references the silver-gilt ceiling. Throughout the house, bathroom floors are made of stone inlaid with sea-life imagery including a sea horse, a snail, and the scallop shell seen here in the expanse of the blue celeste floor.

Even in a transitional space like this upstairs hall off the sitting room, we reference the British-colonial inspiration and the sea with a group of convex mirrors over a Portuguese quill table and an Elizabeth Eakins runner inspired by nineteenth-century sailor's valentines. Those references continue in the sitting room with an Anglo-Indian coffee table, tole tea canisters, brass weights, and other accessories. The lamps are covered in shagreen and the throw pillows have a nautical knot. Coral embroidered curtains are the finishing touch.

In a guest room and connecting loggia, a period colonial bed of ebonized wood helped us pivot the palette into a new color scheme of black and marine blue. The bed adds drama against the Vietnamese bark papered walls. Using black in the tropics may seem counterintuitive, but it's like wearing a black belt: black helps tie everything together.

In another guest room, the walls are upholstered in a floral of white and turquoise embroidered in Mumbai. The stenciled palm tree pillow, coral relief on the fireplace, and fanciful shell sconces evoke the tropical setting.

In the lower level of the house, games and leisure are the siren calls. A display of vintage golf clubs is adjacent to a 40-foot indoor putting green. The poker room overlooks the wine room. There is also a disco room and a photo booth for late-night parties.

In the bar and billiards room, the pattern of the upholstered walls echoes the design and scale of the articulated ceiling. The batik-inspired fabric is reminiscent of textiles that might be found in Southeast Asia. The stools are upholstered in ocean-blue leather and the pool table felt is the color of sand. Nestled under the stairs is a five-foot-tall elephant acquired at Sotheby's, which the owners affectionately nicknamed "Ellie."

OPPOSITE, RIGHT, AND OVERLEAF: In the largest loggia on the back of the house toward the pool, the walls are covered with shells. Even the ceiling medallions are constructed of shells. And back inside, a powder room has paneled shell walls and a silver-gilt grotto-style Italian bench.

265

Terraces, loggias, and
pergolas invite guests
to enjoy the pool
and the ocean beyond.

266

PROJECT CREDITS

Let me first offer enormous thanks to my four incredibly talented partners Lee Cavanaugh, Sarah Ramsey, Claire Ratliff, Alyssa Urban, some of whom have been with me for twenty years (the newbies are only twelve-year veterans!); to Ellen Chopay, our astute controller who has been with the firm for twenty-four years; and to our exceptional staff: Joe Cavaliere, Amanda Darnell, Dani Mazza, Haydee McCarthy, Tracey Pruzan, Katherine Sutton, Andrea Ashe Tutt, Suzanne Vasile, and Caroline White.

Each home presented here exemplifies the delicate balance between many moving parts: the vital collaboration between the decorators, architects, landscape architects, and contractors. I could not be more appreciative of this synergy, but most of all, for the significant part that everyone on the Cullman & Kravis team has played in brandishing our uncompromising dedication to collaboration and quality.

AT HOME
Project Team: Lee Cavanaugh and Alison Eddy
Architect: John B. Murray Architect, LLC
Design Architect: Charlotte Worthy
Contractor: Silver Lining Interiors, Inc.
Art Consultant: Rachel Carr Goulding, Ruth|Catone
Original photography: Durston Saylor
New photography: Eric Piasecki

DOWNTOWN ECLECTIC
Project Team: Claire Ratliff and Amanda Darnell
Architect: Ferguson & Shamamian Architects, LLP
Contractor: Interior Management, Inc.
Landscape Designer: Plants Specialists
Art Consultant: Kimberly Gould
Photography: Eric Piasecki

TRADITIONAL CHIC
Project Team: Lee Cavanaugh, Alison Eddy, Ali Berkley, and Andrea Ashe Tutt
Architect: John B. Murray Architect, LLC
Project Architect: John Pelligra
Contractor: Peter Cosola, Inc.

Landscape Designer: Edmund Hollander, Hollander Design Landscape Artchitects
Art Consultants: Rachel Carr Goulding, Ruth|Catone
Photography: Josh McHugh

LIVING IN COLOR
Project Team: Alyssa Urban, Katherine Sutton, Dani Mazza, and Lauren Mackenzie Dailey
Architects: Thomas A. Kligerman, Ike Kligerman Barkley
Contractor: The Marker Group
Photography: Eric Piasecki

A NEW LOOK
Project Team: Lee Cavanaugh, Alison Eddy, and Andrea Ashe Tutt
Architect: Elliot Rosenblum Architects
Design Architect: Izumi Shepard
Contractor: Interior Management
Art Consultant: Lorinda Ashe
Photography: Eric Piasecki

POSH PIED-À-TERRE
Project Team: Sarah Ramsey and Caroline White
Architect: John B. Murray Architect, LLC
Contractor: Silver Lining Interiors, Inc.
Art Consultant: Graham & Friedrich, LLC
Photography: Eric Piasecki

SOUTHERN HOSPITALITY
Project Team: Alyssa Urban, Katherine Sutton,
Allison Davis, and Lynn Hancock
Architect: Allan Greenberg Architect
Contractor: R.B. Ratcliff & Associates
Landscape Designer: Deborah Nevins and Associates
Art Consultant: Art Advisory Services, Inc.
Photography: Bjorn Wallander

ROOMS WITH A VIEW
Project Team: Alyssa Urban, Katherine Sutton,
and Dani Mazza
Architect: John B. Murray Architect, LLC
Contractor: Peter Cosola, Inc.
Art Consultants: Rachel Carr Goulding,
Ruth|Catone
Photography: Nick Johnson

CONTEMPORARY CLASSIC
Project Team: Katherine Sutton, Melissa Koch,
and Lee Cavanaugh
Architects: Ferguson & Shamamian Architects, LLP
Project Architects: Tom McManus and Justin Ford
Contractor: Tallman Builders
Art Consultants: Rachel Carr Goulding,
Ruth|Catone
Photography: Michael Partenio

"SOME LIKE IT HOT"
Project Team: Alyssa Urban, Katherine Sutton,
and Dani Mazza
Architect: Charlotte Worthy
Contractor: Vella Interiors
Art Consultants: Rachel Carr Goulding,
Ruth|Catone
Photography: Nick Johnson

OCEANFRONT SOPHISTICATION
Project Team: Alyssa Urban, Katherine Sutton,
Allison Davis, and Lynn Hancock
Architect: Thomas A. Kligerman,
Ike Kligerman Barkley
Contractor: Men at Work
Landscape Designer: Edmund Hollander,
Hollander Design Landscape Architecture
Art Consultants: Rachel Carr Goulding,
Ruth|Catone
Photography: William Waldron

OUTSIDER ART AT HOME
Project Team: Claire Ratliff and Amanda Darnell
Photography: Mark Roskams

A SENSE OF PLACE
Project Team: Claire Ratliff, Sarah Ramsey,
Caroline White, and Amanda Darnell
Architect: Peter Zimmerman Architects, Inc.
Contractors: Griffiths Construction and
the Marker Group
Landscape Designer: Jorge Sanchez,
SMI Landscape Architecture
Art Consultant: Michael Altman
Photography: Eric Piasecki

ACKNOWLEDGMENTS

I am so lucky to work in a profession that I love and to have a career that nurtures my soul and makes every day exciting and satisfying.

I am also the luckiest person in the world to have had the opportunity to work not once but twice with a wonderful dream team! The incredibly positive and rewarding experience of *The Detailed Interior* has been replicated here again, so let me thank all those who made it possible:

Tracey Pruzan, my longtime colleague, brilliant cowriter, and treasured friend.
Elizabeth White, our steadfast and elegant editor.
Jill Cohen, our persistent mentor and savvy strategist.
Doug Turshen, our incredibly creative and artistic book designer.
Steve Turner, our computer wizard of endless resources.
Eric Piasecki, our principal photographer, whose artistry captured many of the projects presented in this book.
Nina Reeves and Ellen Rubin, our wise and enthusiastic publicists.

None of this would have been possible, of course, without our valued clients, who take me and our team on an aesthetic and physical journey, one where we learn something new every day. Thank you for trusting us with your dreams for your homes and your families and for letting us realize your vision.

People always say that it "takes a village" to realize the projects such as those presented in these pages, but truly, I think it would be more accurate to say that it takes a metropolis. Here are just a few of our talented and most beloved collaborators and vendors: A&R Asta, Jean Alliaume, Joe Beam, Beauvais, Charles Beckley, Anthony Lawrence Belfair, Francesca Bettridge, E. Braun, Crosby Street Studios, M. Gabaree, Holland & Sherry, Lamptouch, Larrea, Lesage, Lowy, Paul Maybaum, MTS Express, MZ Movers, Penn & Fletcher, Phoenix, Pintura, Platypus, Ranjit Ahuja, Remains Lighting, Eli Rios, Daniel Scuderi, Stark, Sterling, Alan Thorp, Mark Uriu, Gabe Velazquez, Collier Webb, Dave Williams, and Steve Williams.

Thank you so much to the magazine editors, writers, and bloggers who continue to recognize and support our work over all these many years. I must thank especially Amy Astley, Stacey Bewkes, Michael Boodro, D. J. Carey, Sophie Donelson, Alison Levasseur, Paige Rense, Robert Rufino, Margaret Russell, Susanna Salk, Clinton Smith, Jacqueline Terrebone, and Newell Turner.

And, needless to say, I could never have gotten here without my supportive husband, Edgar, and my three children, Trip, Sam, and Georgina. And in the same breath, I would like to salute my late partner, Hedi Kravis, who passed away in 1997. Somehow, she convinced me (and our early clients) to start a business about which we didn't know too much at the outset! Thank goodness, it just worked!

Each member of this creative endeavor is responsible for a critical and interrelated piece of the puzzle of design—and of my life—and I am thankful for all of you, every day.

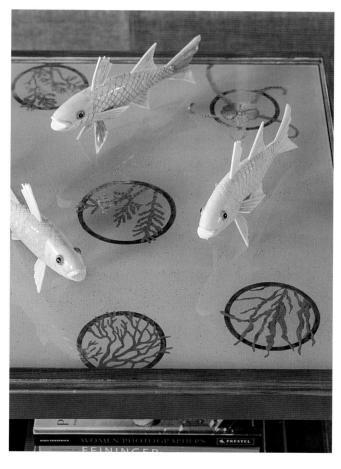

Copyright © 2017 Elissa Cullman and Tracey Pruzan

First published in the United States by The Monacelli Press

All rights reserved.

Library of Congress Control Number 2017932811

ISBN 9781580934961

Designed by Doug Turshen with Steve Turner

Printed in China

The Monacelli Press
6 West 18th Street
New York, New York 10010